Japanese Snacks

get started
making

Japanese
Snacks

step-by-step recipes
for delectable bites

Yamashita Masataka

Marshall Cavendish
Cuisine

Chef Yamashita Masataka was trained in Tsuji Culinary Institute, a well-known and respected culinary institute in Osaka, Japan. He worked at various pâtisseries around Japan before starting his own pâtisserie in Nara.

The pâtisserie quickly became one of the top in Nara. Eight years later, yearning for new challenges and a change of scenery, chef Yamashita moved to Singapore where he took charge of the kitchen at Pâtisserie Glacé, turning it into a haven for delightful cakes and pastries. Chef Yamashita soon saw an opportunity to revive his pâtisserie from Japan and re-established Flor Pâtisserie.

Today, chef Yamashita no longer runs Flor, but his own Japanese artisan pâtisserie at Tanjong Pagar Plaza, aptly named Chef Yamashita.

The recipes in this book were taken from chef Yamashita's cookbook, *Tanoshii Wagashi*, featuring delicate Japanese confections known as *wagashi*.

www.chefyamashita.com
www.facebook.com/chefyamashita

To my beloved Ami.
Thanks for always being by
my side through thick and thin
—we finally have our very own
shop in Singapore!

Contents

ICHIGO DAIFUKU • 38
Strawberry Red Bean Mochi

SATSUMAIMO TO RINGO NO CHAKIN • 42
Sweet Potato & Apple Chakin

AZUKI PANNAKOTTA • 46
Red Bean Panna Cotta

KABUCHA PUDDING • 50
Pumpkin Pudding

YUKIDAMA COOKIES • 54
Snowball cookies

KABOCHA FINANSHE • 58
Pumpkin Financiers

Introduction

As a chef from Nara, Japan, I was professionally trained in Japanese baking styles. The techniques I learned fascinated me. All these years, creating beautiful, delicious cakes and sweets for others has been my greatest passion. I believe I can bring much happiness to those around me through the pastries that I make. And I believe you can do the same.

Wagashi refers to traditional Japanese sweets. In this book, I have specially come up with a selection of traditional and modern Japanese-style sweets, which I hope you will enjoy. I always believe that with sufficient guidance, baking can be a fun and enjoyable experience for everyone. That is why during the months of putting together this book, I carefully selected the recipes to make sure each one is easy to follow. Even if you are a novice in the kitchen, the techniques involved are friendly and manageable.

The ingredients used in this book are not hard to find and are available at local supermarkets and baking supply stores in Singapore. The recipes also do not require special equipment—simple pots, bowls, baking trays, spoons, spatulas and a whisk—will be enough to create these Japanese treats with fun and ease.

With this new cookbook in your hands, it is now time to try out the recipes! I encourage you to have fun while doing so and not to worry if things don't work out the first time. Familiarise yourself with the recipe and try again.

I am deeply grateful that you are buying my book, but the greater joy comes when I know you have tried out my suggestions and succeeded in making what you like. I am sure it will also bring your loved ones much happiness to try what you have created or join you in the process of making *wagashi*.

I wish you a joyful time filled with beautiful *wagashi* that you will now be able to create by yourself in your own kitchen.

Chef Yamashita Masataka

Some of the ingredients used in the recipes can be found in Japanese supermarkets and baking supply stores.

Azuki

Azuki beans can be red, green, yellow or white, but the name is now most commonly associated with the red beans. Azuki beans can be used in both sweet and savoury preparations, but they are mainly enjoyed in desserts.

Shiratama Flour

Like mochi flour, *shiratama* flour is milled from *mochigome*, but it goes through a different process of soaking and grinding, and is sold as granules rather than powder. *Shiratama* flour produces *wagashi* that has a more refined texture than mochi flour.

Kuzu Powder

Also known as *kuzu* starch or *kuzu* root powder, this superior starch is derived from the root of the *kuzu* plant. It is used as a thickening agent in stews and gravies, and also in making Japanese *wagashi*. It gives Japanese sweets such as *kuzu kiri* its translucent quality and firmess.

Japanese Black Sugar

Also known as *kurozatou*, this pure cane sugar originates from Okinawa. It is rich in minerals and vitamins and has a complex molasses flavour that is salty, bitter and sweet. It is available as irregularly shaped pieces and in powder form.

Japanese Custard Sugar

Also known as *johakutou*, this white cane sugar is popularly used in Japanese baking and in making *wagashi*. It is a very fine, soft sugar, and it is used to give a moist sweetness to Japanese sweets. Castor sugar can be used as a substitute, but the final product with not be as moist.

Kinako

This fragrant, nutty-tasting powder is made from roasted soy beans. It is often used as a coating for *wagashi*, and is increasingly also used to flavour other confections such as cookies and ice cream.

Japanese
Bean
Pastes

TSUBU-AN
Whole Red Bean Paste

Makes about 450 g

~~~~~~~~~~~~~~ Ingredients ~~~~~~~~~~~~~~

Azuki **(red beans)** 300 g,
  soaked overnight

Water as needed

Japanese custard sugar
  260 g

Salt a pinch

1. Drain the beans and place into a 20-cm wide pot with 600 ml water. Bring to the boil over high heat. When the water is boiling, add 200 ml cold water to the pot. Let the water return to the boil, then remove from heat. Drain and rinse the beans.

2. Return the beans to the pot and add 850 ml water. Bring to the boil over high heat. When the water is boiling, lower the heat and simmer for 40–60 minutes until the beans are tender. Add more water if necessary.

3. Drain the beans and return to the pot. Place over low heat. Add half the sugar and stir constantly with a spatula until the sugar is melted.

4. Add the remaining sugar and salt and continue stirring until the beans leave the sides of the pot. Test if the paste is ready by lifting the paste with the spatula. It should hang down and form a triangular shape. Continue cooking for another few minutes if necessary.

5. Store *tsubu-an* in small portions and use as needed. *Tsubu-an* will keep for 2–3 days in the refrigerator or up to 1 week in the freezer.

KOSHI-AN
Fine Red Bean Paste

makes about 300 g

~~~~~~~~~~~~~~~~~~ Ingredients ~~~~~~~~~~~~~~~~~~

Azuki (red beans) 250 g,
soaked overnight and
drained

Water as needed

Japanese custard sugar
240 g

Salt 1/4 tsp

1. Place the beans in a pot and cover with water. Bring to the boil over medium heat. When the water is boiling, add 50 ml cold water to the pot. Let the water return to the boil, then remove from heat. Drain and rinse the beans.

2. Repeat the above process of boiling the beans another two times. When boiling the beans for the third time, lower the heat and let simmer for about an hour. Add more water gradually as it boils down, keeping the beans submerged.

3. Test if the beans are ready by pressing a bean between your fingers. It should be soft enough to be easily crushed. Continue to simmer if the beans are still not soft enough.

4. Press the beans through a coarse sieve into a mixing bowl half-filled with water. Discard the skins. Let the mixture sit until the water separates from the paste. Using a small ladle, gently strain off and discard the water.

5. Transfer the paste to a bowl lined with a clean cotton cloth. Twist the cloth to squeeze out all the water from the paste.

6. Place the paste in a pot over low heat. Add half the sugar and mix until the sugar is melted. Add the remaining sugar and salt.

7. Stir constantly until the sugar is melted and the paste leaves the sides of the pot. Test if the paste is ready by lifting with the spatula. It should hang down and form a sticky triangular shape. If it does not, continue to stir over low heat for another few minutes and test again.

8. Transfer the paste to an aluminium tray and let cool in the refrigerator.

9. Store *koshi-an* in small portions and use as needed. *Koshi-an* will keep for 2–3 days in the refrigerator or up to 1 week in the freezer.

DORAYAKI
Pancakes with Red Bean Paste

Makes about 4 dorayaki

~~~~~~~~~~~~~~~~~~~~ Ingredients ~~~~~~~~~~~~~~~~~~~~

Eggs 2, medium

Japanese custard sugar
120 g

Honey 15 g

Baking powder ¹/₄ tsp

Water 60 ml

Pastry flour 130 g, sifted

Salad oil as needed

Koshi-an (page 18)
180–200 g, divided into
8 equal portions and rolled
into balls

1. Crack the eggs into a large bowl and whisk lightly. Add the sugar and whisk until the mixture is pale. Add the honey and whisk again.

2. Mix the baking powder with the water and add to the bowl.

3. Add the pastry flour, making sure there are no lumps.

4. Heat a frying pan to 180–200°C and brush with oil. Lower the heat and test if the pan is at the right temperature by dropping a small drop of batter (about 1.5 cm diameter) into the pan. When the batter starts to bubble, flip it over and check the colour on the other side. Repeat until the batter turns golden brown. The pan should be at the correct temperature for making the *dorayaki*.

5. Pour a tablespoonful of batter into the frying pan, ensuring that the shape is regular and round.

6. When the batter starts to bubble, flip the pancake over. Cook for about 30 seconds, then remove from the frying pan. Place the pancake lighter side up on a wire rack to cool. Repeat until the batter is used up.

7. Sandwich a portion of *koshi-an* between two pancakes to form a *dorayaki*. Serve.

8. *Dorayaki* can be stored in the freezer for up to 3 days. Thaw in the chiller for 3–4 hours before serving, or warm in a toaster oven.

TIP

For evenly coloured and round pancakes, let the batter fall from the spoon into the pan from a single point, and do not swirl the pan. See photo 5.

DAIGAKU IMO
Honey-glazed Sweet Potatoes

Makes 3–4 servings

~~~~~~~~~~~ Ingredients ~~~~~~~~~~~

Sweet potatoes 250 g

Canola oil 15 ml

Black sesame seeds
$^1/_4$ tsp

SAUCE

Japanese custard sugar
30 g

Honey 20 g

Light soy sauce 7.5 ml

Water 30 ml

Canola oil 15 ml

1

2

3

4

1. Wash and scrub the sweet potatoes well as they will be cooked with the skin on. Cut into bite-size pieces.

2. Place the sweet potatoes on a microwave-safe plate and cook in a microwave oven on Medium-High for about 6 minutes. Test that the sweet potato is cooked by piercing with a bamboo skewer. The bamboo skewer should go through easily. Cook the sweet potato for another minute if necessary.

3. Heat the oil in a saucepan over medium heat. Add the sweet potatoes and cook until they start to brown. Transfer to a plate.

4. Place all the ingredients for the sauce in the saucepan and stir over low heat until well mixed and the sauce is a little sticky. Return the sweet potatoes to the pan. Mix to coat each piece well with the sauce.

5. Transfer to a plate and sprinkle with black sesame seeds. Serve.

6. *Daigaku-imo* can be stored in an airtight container in the refrigerator for up to 2 days. Reheat in a toaster oven before consuming.

KARINTOU
Deep-fried Black Sugar Sticks

Makes 45–50 pieces

~~~~~~~ Ingredients ~~~~~~~

Bread flour 75 g

Pastry flour 25 g

Salt $^1/_8$ tsp

Japanese custard sugar 5 g

Baking powder $^1/_6$ tsp

Water $^1/_6$ tsp + 50 ml

Canola oil as needed

SYRUP

Japanese black sugar 60 g

Cornflour 7 g

Water 20 ml

1. Sift the bread flour, pastry flour, salt and sugar into a mixing bowl.

2. Mix the baking powder with $1/6$ tsp water in a small bowl and add to the mixing bowl. Add another 50 ml water and knead to get a smooth dough. Cover with plastic wrap and refrigerate for about 30 minutes.

3. Dust a cutting board with some flour. Place the chilled dough on the cutting board and roll into a sheet about 0.3-cm thick.

4. Cut into 5 x 0.3-cm sticks. Keep them slightly apart so they do not stick.

5. Heat sufficient oil for deep-frying in a pan until about 180°C. Gently lower the dough sticks into the hot oil and deep-fry for about 3 minutes or until golden brown. Remove and set aside to drain. Place in a mixing bowl.

6. Prepare the syrup. Mix the black sugar, cornflour and water in a microwave-safe bowl and cook in the microwave oven on High for about 20 seconds. Remove and stir well, then cook for another 30–40 seconds until the mixture starts to bubble and boil, and is sticky.

7. Pour the syrup over the fried dough sticks and mix well. Place the dough sticks on a sheet of baking paper for the syrup to set, keeping them slightly apart so they do not stick.

8. Serve or store in an airtight container for up to 3 days.

MIZUYOUKAN
Sweet Red Bean Paste Jelly

Makes one 20-cm tray

~~~~~~~~~~~~~~~~~~~~~~ Ingredients ~~~~~~~~~~~~~~~~~~~~~~

Agar-agar strips 4 g

Water 500 ml + 40 ml

Japanese custard sugar 200 g

Koshi-an **(page 18)** 300 g

Kuzu **powder** 5 g

Salt a pinch

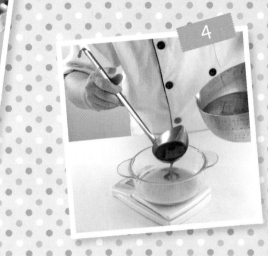

1.   Soak the agar-agar strips in water overnight. Line a 20-cm square tray with baking paper.

2.   Drain the agar-agar strips and place in a small pan. Add 500 ml water and place over high heat. Bring the water to the boil and stir to dissolve the agar-agar. When the agar-agar is dissolved, stir in the sugar.

3.   Pour the contents of the pan through a strainer into a bowl, then return the mixture to the pan. Place over medium heat and add the *koshi-an*. Stir until the *koshi-an* dissolves and the mixture comes to a boil. Remove from heat.

4.   In a bowl, mix the *kuzu* powder with 40 ml water. Stir until the *kuzu* is dissolved. Add 180 ml of the *koshi-an* mixture and mix well.

5.   Pour the *kuzu-koshi-an* mixture into the pan and bring to the boil over medium heat, stirring well with a spatula. Let boil for 3 minutes, stirring all the while. Remove from heat and stir in the salt.

6.   Fill a large heatproof bowl with iced water. Place the pan in the water and stir the mixture slowly to cool it. As the mixture cools, it will become sticky.

7.   Pour the mixture into the prepared tray. Cover and leave to set. When set, refrigerate for about 30 minutes. Cut and serve, or store refrigerated for up to 2 days.

ICHIGO DAIFUKU
Strawberry Red Bean Mochi

Makes 6 pieces

~~~~~~~~~~ Ingredients ~~~~~~~~~~

Strawberries 6

Tsubu-an **(page 14)** 120 g

Potato starch 15 g

Shiratama **flour** 60 g

Water 60 ml + 60 ml

Japanese custard sugar
40 g, sifted

Glucose 1/2 tsp

$\sim\!\sim\!\sim\!\sim\!\sim\!\sim\!\sim\!\sim$ Method $\sim\!\sim\!\sim\!\sim\!\sim\!\sim\!\sim\!\sim$

1. Rinse and hull the strawberries, then pat them dry.

2. Divide the *tsubu-an* into 6 equal portions.

3. Roll a portion of *tsubu-an* into a ball and flatten slightly. Place a strawberry in the centre and bring the *tsubu-an* up to enclose the strawberry. Roll between your palms to form a round. Repeat with the remaining ingredients. Keep covered.

4. Sprinkle an aluminium tray with some potato starch. Set aside.

5. In a glass bowl, mix the *shiratama* flour with 60 ml water. Stir with a spatula until well mixed. Add another 60 ml water and continue to stir. Add the Japanese custard sugar and mix well.

6. Place the *shiratama* mixture in the microwave oven and cook for 1 minute on Medium. Remove and mix, then repeat to cook and mix the mixture another two times. The resulting dough should be translucent and shiny. Use a spatula to mix the dough until it is sticky.

7. Add glucose and stir well.

8. Transfer the dough to the prepared aluminium tray and fold in half. Be careful not to get any potato starch on the top surface of the dough or it will not stick when folded.

9. Cut the dough into 6 equal portions. Shape each portion into a round and flatten slightly. Remove any potato starch on your hands with a brush.

10. Place a wrapped strawberry in the middle of a dough round with the tip of the strawberry facing down. Bring the edges of the dough up around the wrapped strawberry and enclose. Place the *ichigo daifuku* on a serving plate with the strawberry tip facing upwards. Repeat with the remaining ingredients.

11. Serve immediately.

3

5

8

10

SATSUMAIMO TO RINGO NO CHAKIN
Sweet Potato & Apple Chakin

Makes 16–18 pieces

~~~~~~~~~~~~~~~~~~~~ Ingredients ~~~~~~~~~~~~~~~~~~~~

Sweet potatoes 300 g

Salt a pinch

Apple 100 g

Japanese custard sugar 20 g

Mixed fruit 30 g

Fresh cream 30 ml

TIP

The mixed fruit adds colour to the dumplings. Use only red or green glacé cherries or raisins to adjust the colour as desired. Vary it according to the colour theme of your party!

1. Peel the sweet potatoes and cut into 2-cm cubes. Wrap in aluminium foil and cook in the toaster oven for about 30 minutes, or until tender.

2. Place the sweet potatoes in a mixing bowl. Mash while still warm. Season with salt and set aside to cool.

3. Core the apple and slice thinly. Place in a pan over low heat. Add sugar and cook, stirring, for 15 minutes.

4. Add the cooked apple to the sweet potato mash. Mix well.

5. Mix the mixed fruit with the cream. Add to the sweet potato mash and mix again.

6. Line a small bowl with plastic wrap and spoon in 20 g of the sweet potato mixture.

7. Twist the plastic wrap and shape the mixture into a tight dumpling.

8. Repeat to make more dumplings until the mash is used up. Refrigerate for about 30 minutes.

9. Unwrap the dumplings and arrange on a serving plate. Serve immediately or store in an airtight container for up to 2 days.

AZUKI PANNAKOTTA
Red Bean Panna Cotta

Makes 4–5 servings

~~~~~~~~~~~~~~~~~~~~ Ingredients ~~~~~~~~~~~~~~~~~~~~

Leaf gelatin 5 g

Milk 150 ml

**Japanese custard
sugar** 20 g

Koshi-an (page 18) 80 g

Fresh cream 100 ml

1. Place the leaf gelatin in a bowl of iced water to soften. Set aside.

2. Pour the milk into a pan and heat to 70°C.

3. Remove the gelatin from the iced water and squeeze out the excess water. Add to the heated milk. Add the sugar and mix until both the sugar and gelatin are dissolved and the milk is cool.

4. Stir in the *koshi-an* and cream.

5. Pour the mixture into 4–5 small moulds and refrigerate for 30 minutes.

6. Unmould the panna cotta and serve.

7. If not serving immediately, leave the panna cotta in the moulds and store refrigerated for up to 2 days.

KABUCHA PUDDING
Pumpkin Pudding

Makes 6 small puddings

~~~~~~~~~~~~~~~~~~~~~~ Ingredients ~~~~~~~~~~~~~~~~~~~~~~

Pumpkin 280 g

Eggs 3, medium

Japanese custard sugar 80 g

Fresh cream 200 ml

Milk 300 ml

CARAMEL

Water 20 ml

Japanese custard sugar 160 g

Hot water 20 ml

~~~~~~~~~ Method ~~~~~~~~~

1. Preheat the oven to 170°C. Prepare 6 ramekins, each about 7.5-cm wide.

2. Prepare the caramel. Place the water and sugar in a small saucepan over medium heat. Stir constantly with a wooden spatula until the mixture is golden brown. Add the hot water gradually while stirring until well-mixed.

3. Spoon 1 tsp of the warm caramel into each ramekin. Place on a roasting pan and set aside.

4. Cut the pumpkin into 8 even pieces with the skin on. Place the pumpkin in the microwave oven and cook on High for about 5 minutes until the pumpkin is tender.

5. Peel the pumpkin and place in a food processor with the eggs, sugar, cream and half the milk. Process until smooth. Pour the pumpkin mixture into a glass bowl.

6. In a small saucepan, heat the remaining 150 ml milk to about 65°C. Add to the pumpkin mixture and mix well.

7. Ladle the pumpkin mixture into the prepared ramekins. Fill the roasting pan with hot water to come halfway up the sides of ramekins. Bake for 30–35 minutes until pudding is set. Serve immediately.

YUKIDAMA COOKIES
Snowball cookies

Makes 18–20 small cookies

~~~~~~~~~~~ Ingredients ~~~~~~~~~~~

Unsalted butter 60 g

Pastry flour 100 g, sifted

Japanese custard sugar
 20 g

Walnuts 20 g, finely chopped

Icing sugar 30 g

Kinako (soy bean powder)
 30 g

1. Place a small saucepan over low heat. Add the butter and let it melt. Pour into a glass mixing bowl. Add the flour, sugar and walnuts and mix well into a dough.

2. Roll the dough into a long cylinder about 2-cm in diameter.

3. Cut into two equal lengths. Cut each length into 8–10 pieces. Roll each piece into a ball.

4. Place the balls on a lined baking tray. Cover and set aside in the freezer for about 30 minutes.

5. Preheat the oven to 170°C and bake the cookies for 15 minutes. Set aside to cool.

6. Mix the icing sugar with the *kinako* and dust the cookies before serving.

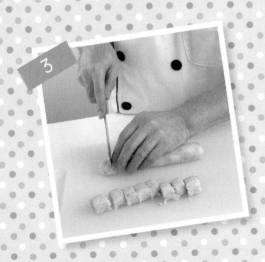

KABUCHA FINANSHE
Pumpkin Financiers

Makes 10-12 small cakes

~~~~~~~~~~~~~~~ Ingredients ~~~~~~~~~~~~~~~

Pastry flour 20 g

Baking powder 2 g

Ground cinnamon 2 g

Almond powder 20 g

Unsalted butter 100 g

Pumpkin 80 g

Japanese black sugar 40 g

Egg whites 90 g

1. Preheat the oven to 200°C. Prepare a financier mould.

2. Sift the pastry flour, baking powder and cinnamon into a mixing bowl. Add the almond powder and mix well. Set aside.

3. Place a pan over low heat. Add the butter and let it melt. Set aside.

4. Cut the pumpkin into small cubes. Place in a microwave-safe bowl and cook in the microwave oven on High for 3–5 minutes, or until tender.

5. Mash the pumpkin while warm. Add the black sugar and mix well with a whisk.

6. Add the egg whites gradually and mix well.

7. Add the flour mixture and mix to incorporate.

8. Add the melted butter and mix again.

9. Spoon the batter into the prepared financier mould and bake for about 17 minutes or until cakes are risen and golden. Set aside to cool before serving.

TIP

The pumpkin need not be peeled as the skin is edible. Mash it together with the yellow flesh.

Weights & Measures

Quantities for this book are given in Metric and American (spoon and cup) measures. Standard spoon and cup measurements used are: 1 teaspoon = 5 ml, 1 tablespoon = 15 ml and 1 cup = 250 ml. All measures are level unless otherwise stated.

LIQUID AND VOLUME MEASURES

Metric	Imperial	American
5 ml	$1/6$ fl oz	1 teaspoon
10 ml	$1/3$ fl oz	1 dessertspoon
15 ml	$1/2$ fl oz	1 tablespoon
60 ml	2 fl oz	$1/4$ cup (4 tablespoons)
85 ml	$2^{1}/_2$ fl oz	$1/3$ cup
90 ml	3 fl oz	$3/8$ cup (6 tablespoons)
125 ml	4 fl oz	$1/2$ cup
180 ml	6 fl oz	$3/4$ cup
250 ml	8 fl oz	1 cup
300 ml	10 fl oz ($1/2$ pint)	$1^{1}/_4$ cups
375 ml	12 fl oz	$1^{1}/_2$ cups
435 ml	14 fl oz	$1^{3}/_4$ cups
500 ml	16 fl oz	2 cups
625 ml	20 fl oz (1 pint)	$2^{1}/_2$ cups
750 ml	24 fl oz ($1^{1}/_5$ pints)	3 cups
1 litre	32 fl oz ($1^{3}/_5$ pints)	4 cups
1.25 litres	40 fl oz (2 pints)	5 cups
1.5 litres	48 fl oz ($2^{2}/_5$ pints)	6 cups
2.5 litres	80 fl oz (4 pints)	10 cups